EXPLAINING
Grace
Undeserved Favour, Irresistible Force or Unconditional Forgiveness?

DAVID PAWSON

ANCHOR RECORDINGS

First published in Great Britain in 2016 by
Anchor Recordings Ltd
Synegis House, 21 Crockhamwell Road,
Woodley, Reading RG5 3LE

**For more of David Pawson's teaching,
including DVDs and CDs, go to
www.davidpawson.com**

**FOR FREE DOWNLOADS
www.davidpawson.org**

**For further information,
email: info@davidpawsonministry.com**

ISBN 978-1-909886-84-1

Printed by Lightning Source

This booklet is based on a talk. Originating as it does from the spoken word, its style will be found by many readers to be somewhat different from my usual written style. It is hoped that this will not detract from the substance of the biblical teaching found here.

As always, I ask the reader to compare everything I say or write with what is written in the Bible and, if at any point a conflict is found, always to rely upon the clear teaching of scripture.

David Pawson

EXPLAINING
Grace
Undeserved Favour, Irresistible Force or Unconditional Forgiveness?

What is grace?

There are three different understandings of grace which are widespread in the church today. One of them I believe to be the truth, and I believe the other two are errors that are misleading people. I'll give you the three understandings straight away and then we will think about each one. The first understanding of grace defines it as *undeserved favour*. That, I believe, is the biblical understanding. The second is that grace is an *irresistible force* – that God uses grace to force you against your will to be one of his family. The third understanding of grace is *unconditional forgiveness*. It is those last two that I believe are a misunderstanding of biblical grace. Interestingly, in 2013 when I was in Jakarta, Indonesia I found that the main misunderstanding seems to be the middle one – that grace is an irresistible force. In Singapore, the third seemed to be the major problem: the "unconditional forgiveness" understanding of grace.

Let us begin with the scriptural understanding. "Grace" is a beautiful word, but in English it has too many meanings. I will give you a funny one straightaway. I was born in the county of Northumberland. Off the coast there are some islands called the Farne Islands. On the outer part of those islands there are a lot of very dangerous rocks. A famous

5

lighthouse had been built to warn ships about them. At the end of the nineteenth century the lighthouse keeper was a man called Darling, who had a daughter in her late teens called Grace. She became one of the most famous women in Britain in the Victorian era because she looked out of the lighthouse window one day and saw a steamship that had grounded on the rocks and was breaking up. A few members of the crew had managed to scramble onto another rock. But the storm was very great and the huge waves were crashing over the rocks. She persuaded her father to get out a rowing boat, and she and her father rowed that boat half a mile to the wreck, saving the lives of the people on the rock. Headlines in the newspapers across the whole nation read "Saved by Grace" – and they meant Grace Darling. That became a sort of byword for our whole nation at that time.

I am going to refer to being "saved by grace", but not by Grace Darling! However we use the word in English for so many other things. We use it of ballet dancers, and we say, "They are very graceful," meaning they move with beauty. Then, if we owe money and we can't pay it by the date due we may ask for seven days' grace, meaning we want more time to pay it. Or if we have to finish a job and we haven't done so within the agreed period we might say, "Please give me some grace," meaning a little extra time to complete the job. So we use it for so many different meanings. We use it even for a pleasing or a redeeming quality in an otherwise not very attractive personality. We say, "That's his redeeming grace." So those meanings in use of the English word "grace" really don't help us.

Then again, we say it as a short prayer before a meal. "Will somebody say grace?" I don't know how the word got into that. When you meet a Duke or a Duchess they have the title "Your Grace". Archbishops of the Church of England are formally addressed as "Your Grace". I am reminded of another funny story when a vicar had invited the Archbishop to come for lunch after he had been preaching one Sunday in the church. The vicar told his family, "Now you must remember before you address the Archbishop you must say, 'Your Grace.'" So when the bishop came in and was introduced to his little girl she said, "For what we are about to receive may the Lord make us truly thankful."

This is the mixed bag of meanings that has been poured into this word, but we want the biblical meaning. "Grace" is a lovely word, occurring twenty times in the New Testament. Of those, sixteen are from St. Paul, so we know that it is a word that had special meaning for him. We get the full flavour of it from his writings. On the whole, evangelical Christians build their gospel primarily on Paul's teaching. Therefore grace is a word that is very commonly used by them. It is only used once in the Gospel of Luke about Jesus as a boy – that grace was upon him. But on the whole it is used about God the Father who is the God of grace and, more often, about the grace of our Lord Jesus Christ. Occasionally the Holy Spirit is called the Spirit of grace. But nearly all Paul's usage of the term applies to the second person of the Trinity: the grace of our Lord Jesus Christ.

In the Bible there is no such thing as "grace" without its being *embodied in a person*. You can't point to just anything and say "That's grace" – just as there is no such "thing" as love, you can only find it in *persons*. Grace clearly exists in all three persons of the Trinity. It is not used as an adjective (gracious) in the Bible. It is used always as a noun. Do remember that it doesn't exist by itself. When you sing a hymn like *Amazing Grace* it sounds as if it is a separate thing that does all that for you, but it is not. I underline this point: *grace doesn't exist except in persons; it does exist supremely in our Lord Jesus Christ.*

What does it mean? Why do we use it of him primarily?

Well there is one secular use of the term that gives us a clue. In England, the Crown owns a number of properties, some of which are leased out rent-free to members of the Royal Family and friends of the Queen. These homes are called "grace and favour" residences. That is using the word "grace" properly. Very closely related to the word "gift", it refers to something given away free. So a grace and favour residence is a house rent-free for you, a gift from the monarch. That is the real meaning. It is a favour done for someone else as a free gift.

But we must go on from that. It has other kinds of flavours with it that bring it alive. The biggest flavour of the word "grace" is that it is *a free gift given to people who don't deserve it*. In a way, the people who get a grace and favour residence from the Queen may deserve it because they are relatives of hers or have become close friends and this is their reward. But grace is not a reward; it is totally different from a wage which you have earned. No one can earn grace; no one can merit it.

But it is even more startling than that. *Grace is not only offered to people who don't deserve it, it is offered to people who have done everything not to deserve it.* The grace of our Lord Jesus Christ is offered to those who are his enemies. It was while we were his enemies that Christ died for us. Not only did we not earn it, we really had done everything not to deserve it. It is given to the worst people. That is grace. That gives the grace of our Lord Jesus Christ a unique flavour. There has never been anyone like him who has given so much to the worst people who have done everything not to deserve it. Therefore he is the supreme example of grace and favour, and his is an undeserved favour. That is the essence of this beautiful word "grace".

It has another flavour attached to it: it takes the initiative, it creates a relationship and it takes the first step in creating that relationship. There is an initiative in grace in that God loved us before we loved him, and Christ died for us before we ever felt the need of anyone to do that. That is grace and it became a benediction, a blessing, in the early church: "The love of God, the grace of our Lord Jesus, and the fellowship of the Spirit...." It is still used in many churches in that way. What a blessing it is to know the love of God, the grace of our Lord Jesus and the fellowship of the Holy Spirit. That is the most blessed life you can have.

What response to grace is appropriate? The answer is gratitude, thankfulness. It is interesting that the words "grace" and "gratitude" are related, and that another related word is "gratuity". When you pay a taxi driver or a waiter who has served you, maybe you add a tip, sometimes called a gratuity, which is a free gift. Very occasionally, even in scripture, the word "grace" is applied to human beings who show gratitude for the grace they have received. In the Greek language the same applies. The word "grace" in Greek is *charis*. I am sure you have heard of the word "charismatic", which is based on the Greek word "charismata", meaning the free gifts of the Spirit. The Greek word for "thank you" is *eucharisteo* and that has led many churches to call their celebration of the Lord's Supper a "Eucharist" – which is a very big thank you to God the Father for sending Jesus to die for us. Sometimes they say it and sometimes they sing it. You see on the notice boards of some churches, "Sung Eucharist 11 a.m. Sunday Morning".

So the appropriate response to grace is gratitude and the word "grace" is rarely applied to human beings, but when it is it means a very thankful person overflowing with gratitude to God for the grace of his Son.

Why did Paul in his letters major on the word "grace"? Because if ever there was an example of grace it was Paul. When we first encounter him in the Bible he is breathing out slaughter against the Christians. He has become an anti-Christian missionary. He has left the land of Israel to go after Christians elsewhere. When he stepped outside his own land to go and put Christians in Damascus in prison to try to stop their activities, he was met by Jesus, who said, "Saul, Saul, why are you persecuting me?" Paul might have said, "I'm not persecuting you, Jesus, I'm persecuting your followers." But he soon learned that as much as you do it to the least of his brethren you do it to him.

It was then that his understanding of Christians as the Body of Christ came to birth. He was transformed. Jesus told Paul that he was to go to the Gentiles. But he was to take the good news to them, the gospel of God, not Paul's own ideas. It is amazing how this anti-Christian missionary became the greatest missionary to the Gentiles there has ever been, and we still build our faith on his teaching.

He was such an example of grace. He wasn't one of the twelve apostles. He was one born out of due time—the last of them all, the thirteenth. Yet God included him. What grace God had shown to him, the totally undeserving. I believe that is the reason why Paul uses that word more than anyone else in the whole Bible: *charis*, grace.

Having said that, I must sadly now tell you that this word has been terribly misunderstood and therefore misapplied in churches around the world, even to this day. So let me now move into the more negative side of a teacher's task. The first unbiblical meaning sometimes given to grace is that it is an *irresistible force*. This has a long history. It goes back to Augustine who was bishop of a city called Hippo in North Africa in the fifth century. You have probably heard him called "Saint" Augustine because he was canonised by the Roman Church. You may have heard of his *Confessions*, which is one of the first testimonies given, and it is a wonderful testimony. But his teaching did great damage to the church (both Protestant and Catholic) and has had a tremendous influence on church history and even affects the church today.

Augustine had come from a pagan background, having been brought up in a pagan philosophy. Then he went to hear a preacher in Milan called Ambrose and he came to Christ. But the actual conversion took place while he was in a garden, reading Paul's letter to the Romans. He had been a rather bad lad. He already had a mistress and an illegitimate son and he played around. He acknowledges that in his *Confessions*. But after he had found Christ he famously said that we only find rest when we find him: "Our souls can find no rest until we find it in thee" was his prayer. He left his mistress and made provision for his son. In his early years of ministry everything went well. I am excited to read about it. It was good stuff, and it was what the other early Church Fathers had preached.

Then, halfway through his life, his early philosophical position began to creep into his teaching and change it. In the early years he had taught and believed firmly that Jesus would come back to rule on earth. But in his later years he could not accept that. It was too physical, too earthly. He began to react against his early immoral sex life, and ultimately we owe to him that a whole church believed its clergy should be celibate. He even taught later that sex within marriage is sinful – what he called "concupiscence". I find all this very sad because people who revered him as a Church Father followed his teaching right through.

One of the things he began to teach was that it is legitimate to use force to make people Christians. He built that on a text in the parable of the wedding feast where the owner of the feast said: "If those who are invited don't come in, then go into the highways and the byways and *compel* people to come in." It is not a good translation – the word really means to *persuade* them. But he took it quite literally—compel them, make them come in, force them to come in. Grace is then thought of as God's force which he used against our will to establish his kingdom on earth.

Jesus did not allow his servants to fight; they were not to use force to spread the faith. But there came such things as the Spanish Inquisition, which tortured people until they accepted Jesus – especially Jews. From the teaching of Augustine eventually came the Crusades where soldiers set off to Jerusalem to free the Holy Land pilgrimage sites from the Muslim invader, killing Jews on the way.

So a whole lot followed from that teaching about grace as an irresistible force. He didn't actually call it that. That came rather later with the Protestant Reformers. I apologise for all this history, but I think you need to know it to understand what is happening. Later, in the sixteenth century, the Protestant Reformers fed on Augustine's teaching, including his later ideas. Martin Luther was an Augustinian monk, and therefore steeped in Augustine. In Geneva, Calvin wrote two huge volumes entitled *The Christian Institutes*. They are virtually Augustine's teaching brought up to date; they are solid Augustinianism. So the Protestant Reformers were directly influenced by Augustine's understanding of grace.

We now blame Calvin more than we should for spreading that through the churches. What happened was Calvin followed Augustine in many ways, but Calvin died and was followed by his successor in Geneva called Theodore Beza, who took Calvin's teaching to an extreme and taught ultra-Calvinism. He was a key influence in Holland, which became dominated by the Dutch Reformed Church, which is solidly Calvinistic and therefore Augustinian, and so has this teaching of grace. So what Beza taught is what we generally call Calvinism, and I think that is a bit unfair to Calvin.

Now I want to tell you about a Dutchman called Jakob

Hermanszoon. While he was at university the Roman Catholics killed his parents. That is part of the history of Holland; it was a tussle between Protestants and Catholics. He was Protestant and he loved the Lord and he loved scripture. He was asked to be the pastor of the main church in Amsterdam, where the king and queen worshipped. There, I believe, he preached the truth.

While he was at university he changed his name, which is why you may have never heard of Jakob Hermanszoon. It was the habit among students to change their names to Latin ones when they became students. Jakob remembered the name of a German who, centuries earlier, had fought against the Roman invaders and beaten them. So he called himself by the Latin name of that German – Arminius.

Jakob, now known as Arminius, lived such a godly and holy life that no one dared to criticise him while he was alive. But as soon as he was dead some of the Dutch clergy arose and condemned him as a heretic. Few people have read his writings. I have, and I found myself thrilled to bits with his exposition of scripture. Then began a battle between the official Dutch Reformed Church, which was Calvinist, and the followers of Arminius, called Arminians. That tension is still with us and it explains a lot.

After he died, the other clergy called together a synod in the town of Dort (known as the "Synod of Dort"). They produced five basic principles of their Calvinism, each one of which was aimed at denying the teaching of Arminius. Now the five points of Calvinism that you need to know all relate to the five letters of the word "tulip". Holland is famous for its tulips, exporting millions of bulbs around the world. I want you to remember this tulip. It's not the prettiest tulip they have exported. But there are five basic principles they taught to counter the popular preaching of this holy man whom they had never dared to criticise before. Here are the five points of "Calvinism". They should not be called that because Calvin only taught three of them. But Beza added the other two and these are still held by many pastors today:

T is for *total depravity*. That means that we have sunk so low in sin that we have lost all our power to do good, to respond to good, even to accept the gospel. We could never respond to Jesus by ourselves. We can do nothing about our salvation at all; God has to do everything.

U stands for *unconditional election*. This means that God chooses people to be saved and he does not choose them with any regard to the people themselves. He doesn't choose them because they are going to be believers. He doesn't choose them because they are going to be anything. He chooses to save people because he chooses them. He has not told us why he chooses some and not others. He doesn't choose us for anything in us, not even our faith; he chooses us before we believe. In fact, he chooses us and gives us the new birth even before we have repented and believed, because we are so totally depraved we can't repent until we are born again. God leads us to new birth before we know anything about it, then we repent, and then we believe. You may think this is extraordinary teaching, but this is the teaching on grace that is in many churches.

The big question I want to ask a Calvinist is this: how do you explain that some are saved and some are not? Their explanation is that God has chosen some and not others, which means logically that he has chosen some for heaven and chosen some for hell. It is his choice and he has not told us why he has made that choice. It is totally unrelated to us. It means that from our point of view salvation is purely luck; it is purely arbitrary. It is not related to anything in us whatsoever. God has simply chosen one person and not another. That is why this one is saved and not that one.

L stands for *limited atonement*. That is based on the

logic that God would never punish anyone twice for sin, and therefore either he can't send anyone to hell because he has already punished Jesus for their sin, or Jesus didn't die for everybody but only for the elect. Arminius said that Jesus died for everybody. He paid the price for the sins of the whole world. But the Calvinist says, "No he didn't." If he sends anyone to hell after that, he is punishing twice. It is logical. Calvinism is very logical, but not necessarily true.

I is for *irresistible grace*. That is what I mean when I say it is seen as an irresistible force – grace cannot be resisted. If grace decides you will be saved then you will be saved. If grace gets hold of you, you will be kept. It is not dependent on your decision or will or faith – or anything. You will be in heaven because God decided. His force is greater than anything in you.

P stands for *perseverance of the saints*. If God's grace is irresistible then it can keep you against your will. Whatever you do you will end up in heaven because God has chosen you and you can do nothing about that.

Now those are the five things that grew out of grace as an irresistible force. They are the five points of Calvinism. You will find them in the Presbyterian churches. You will find them in what are called the Reformed Churches. You will find those five things, theoretically taught anyway, in a number of the world's Calvinistic denominations, as they are called. I am trying to be as fair as possible. Compel them to come in. God compelled us to be saved, he compels us to be kept, he compels us all the way along the line, and therefore we can use the same compelling people by force to bring them into the kingdom because God wants us to. He would rather have people compelled in than persuaded in. I believe that is a libel on God.

Let us go back to Augustine for a moment. Augustine had someone who opposed him very sharply—a man called

Pelagius. He was a British monk who went to Rome and was alarmed at the corruption in the Church of Rome, with people who were relying on God's force to keep them and were not holy people. They didn't need to be – God's force would get them to heaven! So he reacted against this, too strongly. He went to the opposite extreme and so stressed human responsibility that no room was left for God to do anything. His position was that it is entirely up to you whether you are saved or not – you can save yourself. He would quote Peter on the day of Pentecost who said, "Save yourselves from this corrupt generation." He taught d-i-y (do-it-yourself) salvation, that it is something you do, not God. That was the big argument. I think Augustine was reacting to that extreme.

I thank God that there were some people in the middle of all that. The French bishops said both positions were wrong. They maintained that salvation is the result of human co-operation with the divine. That is nowadays called synergism, meaning "working together". The French bishops were saying: "It is God who saves, but not against our will. We need to respond to grace; we need to receive the gift of grace. When we respond to grace in gratitude and receive the gift of salvation, we are saved. The reason why people are not saved is not because God hasn't chosen them, but because they haven't chosen to receive the gift."

That was their explanation as to why some are saved and some are not. I would stand with the French bishops. I would not stand with Pelagius who said that it is all your doing, and I wouldn't stand with Augustine who said that it is all God's doing. I would say that when a person responds to grace by repenting, believing and receiving, they then begin to be saved.

We could put this difference in a simple picture. Imagine someone being saved from drowning. The Calvinist might say: the man is floating in the water, already dead. He has drowned. He is totally unable to do anything and he needs someone to fish him out of the water and give him the breath of life to save him. That is Calvinism in a nutshell. The Arminian, like those French bishops, could say: the man is not able to swim to the shore, he is drowning and he will be lost, but God throws him the lifebelt – on the end of a rope maybe – and says, "Take hold of this and I'll pull you safely to the shore." Then he will be saved. The latter is the picture of Arminius and I believe that is the picture you get in the New Testament. That is how they preached; repent and believe, and God will pull you to heaven; grab the gospel, get hold of it – that is all you have got to do, but you get hold of it and you will be pulled to safety, and therefore to salvation.

It is the difference between saying "God does it all" and saying "God does it all for the people who respond." Arminius taught that the human response to the grace of God is necessary for salvation, and that is why some are saved and some are not. Some grab hold and find that they are saved. Others will not get hold of it, they turn it down. Simply, according to the Arminian, grace can be refused, but according to Calvin it cannot be refused. In other words, even more simply, you can say yes or no to grace. No one is forced to accept grace. It is an undeserved free gift, but a gift has to be received.

A gift has to be used and relied on. It requires co-operation to become useful and effective. I don't think I can make the point more simply than that. Sooner or later you have to decide if grace means that God does everything and is solely responsible for anybody being saved, or whether it is that some have responded, received the gift, and that it has become theirs and they are very grateful.

When I study my Bible, I see that they were offering grace

but they were demanding repentance and faith. They were demanding a response from people. They were not thinking, "God will save whom he wants to save and that's it." I have many dear friends who are Calvinists and I thank God that some of them keep their Calvinism in the study and don't take it into the pulpit, because when I listen to some of them preach they are preaching a grace that needs to be received. Although in theory they hold that only those who have been chosen by God will receive, they are at least offering the gospel to other people. That is great.

So you had Augustine and Pelagius in tension and each going to an extreme. Later you had Calvinism and Arminianism in tension. I don't think Arminianism went to an extreme, however, in that later tension. But we have inherited two thousand years of church history. If you don't know anything about church history you will be puzzled by the differences between the churches, which is why I have written a book entitled *Where Has the Body Been for 2000 Years?* subtitled "Church History for Beginners".

What happened to the church traditions which had those different understandings? It is interesting to compare what I saw when I visited and taught in both Indonesia and Singapore, in the same region of the world. The Dutch colonised Indonesia, taking with them the Dutch Reformed Church, which is very Calvinistic. That is why you have so many Presbyterian churches in Indonesia today. But Singapore was colonised by the British so there you have, first of all, the Anglican Church, with its white cathedral in the middle of the town. The cathedral itself is modelled on Roman Catholic gothic architecture, which comes from the Middle Ages, because the Church of England is a muddle – but, then again, the British are characteristically in a comprehensive muddle! The Church of England was founded on the fact that King Henry VIII could not get from the Pope a divorce. So he cut himself off from the Pope, made himself head of the Church of England and destroyed every Roman Catholic monastery in England. The Queen is now head of the Church of England in his place. The Church of England decided to settle for a mixture of Catholic and Protestant, but Scotland followed Calvin and the Presbyterians.

The Church of England has some parish churches that are more ritualist than the Roman Catholic Church, and other Anglican churches are plainer than the lowest Protestant. It is an extraordinary mixture. We finish up with high Anglicans, broad Anglicans and low Anglicans. Or, in theological terms: Catholic Anglicans, liberal Anglicans, and evangelical Anglicans. If you study the thirty-nine Articles of Religion of the Church of England, the position is mildly Calvinist, but only mildly – it is on that side of things, but only just. What a mixture that is!

So in the eighteenth century, when the official Church of England was dying spiritually, there arose two brothers, John and Charles Wesley, who led a revival in Britain from which came the Methodist Church. John Wesley had a magazine which he started for his people entitled *The Arminian*. In Singapore, as in many former British colonies, Methodist Arminianism and Anglican mild Calvinism both stem from the British occupation.

I hope that if you are not theologically interested in all this, you are not getting confused, bewildered and shaken in your faith. My prayer is that the Holy Spirit would protect your faith from being confused and disturbed by what I have to teach. But, you see, we inherit two thousand years of church history. Without realising it we have inherited traditions through the different churches. We have inherited different understandings of grace, and that affects your whole thinking. It affects your evangelism. It affects so much else.

In practice, most evangelists are Arminian and preach for a response, believing that if people respond to the gospel they will be saved. Therefore most evangelism is done by people with strong convictions about the first understanding of grace as undeserved favour, a free gift for the very undeserving, but a gift that must be received and used.

We not only need grace at the beginning of the Christian life, we need it all the way through. That is why Paul prayed so much that God would heal him of a physical infirmity that he believed was a handicap to his mission. God said: "No I'm not going to take it away. My grace is sufficient for you, and in your weakness I can be strong." Grace will see you right through to the end. When we have been there a thousand years we will still be singing about it – how undeserved our salvation was. But it wasn't because we did nothing. Theoretically, if someone says to a Calvinist, "What must I do to be saved?" he should be told, "Absolutely nothing. If God has chosen you he will save you," which is why many Calvinists suffer from a loss of assurance. "Has he saved me? Am I sure?" That is awful, if you are not sure whether God has called you – because those who have responded to his call do know that God called them.

Unconditional Forgiveness?

The major problem now, however, is not grace being seen as irresistible force. The problem is an idea of *unconditional forgiveness*. I have to say that this third understanding of grace, which can be found in America, is spreading throughout the world. I came across it all over South Africa when I was there two years before my visit to Singapore, and I asked, "Where did you get all this from?" They said, "Singapore." So I must be honest and share with you what I believe is a misunderstanding of God's beautiful grace when it is interpreted as meaning unconditional forgiveness.

It is good in the sense that it gives God glory for his free grace. But it is bad because it takes that free grace to an extreme teaching in two particulars. First, in teaching that when you come to Christ all your *future* sins are forgiven as well as your past. I cannot find any trace in my Bible of God forgiving sins that have not yet been committed, either before or after conversion. We are not immediately perfect and Christians do sin. But we know what to do about that. In the first letter of John we have very clear instructions: "If we say we have no sin we deceive ourselves. But if we confess our sins he is faithful and just to forgive us our sins, and the blood of Jesus will go on cleansing us from all unrighteousness." That is a promise for Christians. It is written to believers. It tells them that if we sin we have an Advocate in heaven to speak for us, but we need to do our part and we need to confess. When we do so he is faithful and just to *go on* forgiving – that is the tense of the verb, and the blood of Jesus *goes on* cleansing. When a Christian sins we take it to the Lord and get it dealt with; we keep short accounts with God and deal with sin as it arises. We get his dealing with it, his forgiveness, by confessing it.

Now that is a very important passage of scripture. So what do these people who say, "God has forgiven all your future sins" do with that chapter? I was astonished to find they deny that it was written to Christians. They say the first letter of John was written to pagans. But when you read that letter you see that everything in it is clearly addressed to Christians. To twist it and make it something only for pagans is almost laughable, but it is so serious that it is not funny. The new teaching which is *unconditional forgiveness* is denying what scripture is saying.

So the advocates of unconditional forgiveness are teaching this: when you come to Christ all your sins are forgiven – not just everything you have committed in the past but everything you will yet commit in the future, so don't get morbid and think about your sins. That is the kind of teaching that is coming out, and it is tragic teaching. It may make a lot of people happy but it is not the truth. *We can go on being forgiven as long as we confess and ask.* Christians do make mistakes, Christians do fall, but we know it can be dealt with immediately and properly, and sin can be taken away.

Jesus didn't just come to save us from hell, he came to save us from our sins. He came to go on dealing with our sins. He dealt with all our past sins – they were washed away in baptism and that deals with your past. But the one thing John the Baptist was worried about was that while baptism dealt with the past it didn't deal with the future. I can remember my own baptism which was in a dirty green pool, but I felt clean. I knew that my past was washed away. But I can remember vividly the first sin I committed after that. I made the silly mistake of thinking I had undone it all.

Baptism does not deal with your future. That actually needs the baptism of the Holy Spirit. It is no good just having your past cleaned up if you have no help with your future, because, being sinners still, the old man may be dead but he is not lying down. You live in this tension between the old man and the new man. You do sin, but it can be dealt with. 1 John 1 tells you very clearly how to deal with it when it happens. So you don't need to be baptised again – baptism washed your past clean and got you properly started with a new, clean life. Later you will need still to deal with things that hang on and things that come from the pressures of being in a sinful world. But they can be dealt with now – they need to be confessed.

The other thing that follows from this is a downplaying of repentance. Unconditional forgiveness doesn't really depend on repentance. In my understanding of scripture, unrepented sin can't be forgiven – we need to repent first and then that sin can be forgiven. To repent is not just saying sorry. It is doing something. My understanding is that both repentance and faith are things that we *do*. But the mistaken understanding of grace tends to downplay anything that we need to do. So repentance is not often mentioned by such teachers. Yet it was absolutely central to the preaching of Paul.

There is one verse in the New Testament I have never heard a preacher deal with fully. It is the part of Paul's testimony which begins: "I was not disobedient to the heavenly vision...." Most people stop there and I have never heard the rest quoted. It immediately goes on: "so I preached repentance to the Gentiles that they should turn to God and prove their repentance by their deeds." Why don't preachers ever preach this – that repentance is something you prove by your deeds? That is what Paul used to preach. He said to the people of Athens that until then God had winked at their sin – he had overlooked it – but now he commands all men everywhere to repent. That was the apostle's preaching. It was basic. Repent. Repent. Repent.

A young man came to see me. He was on a big motorbike with high handlebars and mirrors stuck out all over the place. I heard him coming a mile off. He stopped at our front door and rang the bell. I opened the door and he said, "I want to talk."

I said, "Well if you want to talk, come on in." He came in, in his black leather clothes covered with brass studs. He sat down on our settee, and it still bears the marks of Paul's visit.

He made himself comfortable and I asked, "What do you want to talk about Paul?"

"I want to be baptised."

"You want to be baptised? Do you know how we baptise people?"

He said, "Yeah, you duck them in the water."

I said, "So you want to be ducked in the water?"

"Yes."

I said, "Paul, do you know what the word 'repent' means?" He said, "Nah, never heard of it."

"Listen carefully, Paul. I want you to go home and I want you to ask Jesus this question: 'Lord Jesus, is there anything in my life that you don't like?' When he tells you something, I want you to cut it out and come back and tell me."

He didn't come back for three weeks. Then I heard the bike again, and there was Paul at the doorstep. So I opened the door and he said, "There."

I said, "What do you mean 'There'?"

"I've stopped biting my nails."

I said, "Right Paul, I'll baptise you now."

He never looked back. He became a great Christian. When you were baptised, were you asked that? I baptise people on proof of repentance, not on profession of faith. That's more biblical: "Repent and be baptised...."

You may laugh at that young man, but when Jesus told him to stop biting his nails he repented and he stopped. That was good enough for me. He learned then that when you are aware of sin you stop it and you deal with it – you repent.

I think that at the root of these two misunderstandings is the fear of the word "works". We are saved by faith not by works. But there is a phrase in the New Testament: "You see that a person is justified by what he does and not by faith alone." That is the Word of God. Notice: "not by faith alone." That is the only place in the Bible where you will find the words "by faith alone", but you find the word "not" in front of them.

Many people think it is by faith alone. It isn't. I was quoting from James 2. But people who have this third misunderstanding of grace don't like the epistle of James one little bit because the key word in James is "do" and they believe that anything we do is what the Bible means by "works". That is not true. Paul was right when he said, "We are not saved by works of the law." Paul was right to say that we are not saved by good works, by good deeds, by trying to be good. But faith has works attached to it – *works of faith*. James also points out that Abraham was justified by faith when he offered Isaac to the Lord. Rahab the prostitute in Jericho was justified by faith when she received the Israelite spies into her home and hid them in a brothel, and then safely sent them out another way back to the Israelite army. The spies of Israel told her, "When we take Jericho, hang a scarlet cord from your window and we'll tell our troops that you're safe." Her house was on top of the wall of Jericho. That is how she could hang a scarlet cord from the window to be seen. So not all the wall of Jericho fell down, one bit of it stayed up, and that was the house of the prostitute Rahab.

In both cases – a good man called Abraham and a bad woman called Rahab – they were justified by faith that acted, faith that *did* something. Whereas again those who take the wrong view of grace tend to say: "Faith is what you say, not what you do. Name it and claim it. Blab it and grab it," or whatever term you use. That is the teaching that goes alongside this misunderstanding of grace.

I think I have probably taught enough on grace to show you what the true understanding is and what the two major false understandings are today. They are very widespread. They are spreading via the internet throughout the world. Everywhere I go to preach I come across them. So please have discernment and recognise these errors which are distorting the truth of God.

We are told in scripture that towards the end of this age the greatest danger for Christians will be deception. We are not deceived just by lies, we are deceived when truth is mixed with error. If the devil told outright lies we would simply say no to him. But he is so clever he deceives people by mixing the truth in with it. The error of grace that I have outlined is often mixed in with the true gospel and with many true things that are being preached with it. The mixture deceives.

That has been true ever since the Garden of Eden. What Satan said to Eve was half true and she swallowed it. He said, "If you take this fruit your eyes will be opened" (and that was true) and "you will be like gods" (which was not true). It was the mixture that fooled Eve, and Adam who was standing by her side, at the same time. Ever since then the devil, who is far cleverer than us, has persuaded people to mix the truths of the gospel with some things that are not true.

It sounds most of the time as if you are listening to the truth, but if you listen carefully there are things being slipped in that have no biblical basis. That is where the danger lies. As we get near the end of time the devil gets more desperate. That is why, five times in just one chapter, when Jesus told us what the end would be signalled by, what to watch for, after each sign he gave them he said "Don't be deceived."

Paul does the same. When he writes to Timothy he says, "This is what will happen in the last days. Men will be lovers of pleasure. People will want preachers who will tickle their ears and tell them what they want to hear. Watch and pray lest you be deceived." When you read the scriptures I am afraid we have to face the fact that it is not all straightforward. The deception will take place inside the church, and tragically, will affect the Christian living of so many people. Go to a church that preaches the truth, the whole truth, and nothing but the truth. Guard your heart against the subtle mixture that deceives and destroys.

ABOUT DAVID PAWSON

A speaker and author with uncompromising faithfulness to the Holy Scriptures, David brings clarity and a message of urgency to Christians to uncover hidden treasures in God's Word.

Born in England in 1930, David began his career with a degree in Agriculture from Durham University. When God intervened and called him to become a Minister, he completed an MA in Theology at Cambridge University and served as a Chaplain in the Royal Air Force for three years. He moved on to pastor several churches, including the Millmead Centre in Guildford, which became a model for many UK church leaders. In 1979, the Lord led him into an international ministry. His current itinerant ministry is predominantly to church leaders. David and his wife Enid currently reside in the county of Hampshire in the UK.

Over the years, he has written a large number of books, booklets, and daily reading notes. His extensive and very accessible overviews of the books of the Bible have been published and recorded in *Unlocking the Bible*. Millions of copies of his teachings have been distributed in more than 120 countries, providing a solid biblical foundation.

He is reputed to be the "most influential Western preacher in China" through the broadcast of his best-selling *Unlocking the Bible* series into every Chinese province by Good TV. In the UK, David's teachings are often broadcast on Revelation TV.

Countless believers worldwide have also benefited from his generous decision in 2011 to make available his extensive audio video teaching library free of charge at www.davidpawson.org and we have recently uploaded all of David's video to a dedicated channel on www.youtube.com

TAKE A LOOK AT YOUTUBE
www.youtube.com/user/DavidPawsonMinistry

THE EXPLAINING SERIES
BIBLICAL TRUTHS SIMPLY EXPLAINED

If you have been blessed reading this book, there are more available in the series. Please register to download more booklets for free by visiting
www.explainingbiblicaltruth.global

Other booklets in the *Explaining* series will include:
The Amazing Story of Jesus
The Resurrection: *The Heart of Christianity*
Studying the Bible
Being Anointed and Filled with the Holy Spirit
New Testament Baptism
How to study a book of the Bible: Jude
The Key Steps to Becoming a Christian
What the Bible says about Money
What the Bible says about Work
Grace – *Undeserved Favour, Irresistible Force
or Unconditional Forgiveness?*
Eternally secure? – *What the Bible says about being saved*
De-Greecing the Church – The impact of Greek thinking
on Christian beliefs
Three texts often taken out of context:
Expounding the truth and exposing error
The Trinity
The Truth about Christmas

They will also be avaiable to purchase as print copies from:
Amazon or **www.thebookdepository.com**

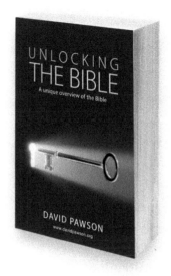

UNLOCKING
THE BIBLE

A unique overview of both the Old and New Testaments, from internationally acclaimed evangelical speaker and author David Pawson. *Unlocking the Bible* opens up the Word of God in a fresh and powerful way. Avoiding the small detail of verse by verse studies, it sets out the epic story of God and his people in Israel. The culture, historical background and people are introduced and the teaching applied to the modern world. Eight volumes have been brought into one compact and easy to use guide to cover both the Old and New Testaments in one massive omnibus edition. *The Old Testament: The Maker's Instructions* (The five books of law); *A Land and A Kingdom* (Joshua, Judges, Ruth, 1&2 Samuel, 1&2 Kings); *Poems of Worship and Wisdom* (Psalms, Song of Solomon, Proverbs, Ecclesiastes, Job); *Decline and Fall of an Empire* (Isaiah, Jeremiah and other prophets); *The Struggle to Survive* (Chronicles and prophets of exile); *The New Testament: The Hinge of History* (Mathew, Mark, Luke, John and Acts); *The Thirteenth Apostle* (Paul and his letters); *Through Suffering to Glory* (Hebrews, the letters of James, Peter and Jude, the Book of Revelation). Already an international bestseller.

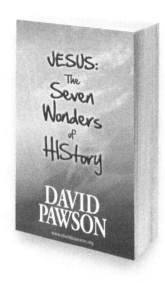

JESUS:
THE SEVEN
WONDERS
OF HISTORY

This book is the result of a lifetime of telling 'the greatest story ever told' around the world. David re-told it to many hundreds of young people in Kansas City, USA, who heard it with uninhibited enthusiasm, 'tweeting' on the internet about 'this cute old English gentleman' even while he was speaking.

Taking the middle section of the Apostles' Creed as a framework, David explains the fundamental facts about Jesus on which the Christian faith is based in a fresh and stimulating way. Both old and new Christians will benefit from this 'back to basics' call and find themselves falling in love with their Lord all over again.

OTHER TEACHINGS
BY DAVID PAWSON

For the most up to date list of David's Books
go to: **www.davidpawsonbooks.com**

To purchase David's Teachings
go to: **www.davidpawson.com**

Lightning Source UK Ltd.
Milton Keynes UK
UKHW020745250822
407828UK00012B/1641